The Circle of Ceridwen Cookery Book(let)

Viking Age Food for Everyday Feasts

Adapted for 21st Century Cooks and Their Kitchens

by Octavia Randolph

Author of The Circle of Ceridwen Saga

The recipes were written by me, and thoroughly tested by Deborah of the blog Deborah Dishes. Deborah is a professional caterer, writer, Romance author, music lover, world traveller, observer of the human condition, and all around Great Sport. And she's funny too. As part of her testing she created a Ninth Century Feast using all of the recipes, and wrote about the experience of cooking, serving, and enjoying the feast in three wonderful blog entries. You can read all about it on her blog, Deborah Dishes. Just search for "A 9th Century Feast".

I've also written of my own dinner party using these recipes. You can find it at www.octavia.net by searching for "My Ninth Century Dinner Party".

The Circle of Ceridwen Saga
Historic Adventure at its Best
Book One is Free at www.octavia.net

Pyewacket Press

ISBN 978 1 942044 24 6
© Octavia Randolph 2019 All Rights Reserved
First Edition October 2014

Book cover design: DesignForBooks.com

I sunk upon a bench and we were brought deep cups of ale and pottery bowls of browis and a wooden platter of wheaten loaves. I did not know if I could eat, but after the first bit of bread I began to feel stronger, and realised how hungry I was. Sidroc ate as if famished, and had more of everything. We drank all the ale and sat next each other on the bench, saying little. I felt the ale and the food and the safety of the place and could not speak any of it, but knew an ease unto pleasure at it all.

> – Ceridwen's first meal on Gotland, from *The Claiming*

Contents

Invitation to Some Enjoyable Eating	1
Honey Cakes	10
Baked Apples (or Pears)	14
Barley Browis	18
Honey-glazed Carrots and Parsnips	22
Oat Griddle Cakes	26
Venison Pie with Juniper Berries	30
Fish Stew with Leeks and Lentils	34
Roasted Fish with Green Sauce	38
Roast Fowl, Two Ways	42
Lavender-scented Pudding	46
Liquid Conversions	54
Weight Conversions	55

The Circle of Ceridwen Cookery Book(let)

Invitation to Some Enjoyable Eating

Writing about food and cooking and eating in my novels has always been a pleasure, one I hope it has been to read as well. Eating in Anglo-Saxon England and in Scandinavia in the late ninth century, the age of *The Circle of Ceridwen Saga*, was circumscribed by at least two factors: The limited ability to preserve any foodstuffs for long, and the comparatively narrow range of edibles available to our ninth century forefathers and foremothers. Think about it: not only were there no out-of season tomatoes; there were no tomatoes at all, as these New World natives had to wait until the Conquistadors of the early 16th century carried them back to Europe from the mountain foothills of South America. The same goes with that later European staple, the potato, brought back to Europe from the Incan empire in the later 16th century. Ditto maize, the American corn. Rice, native to Asia and parts of Africa, was also largely unknown in Europe until its use and cultivation spread from Sicily northward beginning in the 15th century. (The third factor, that of economics, we will address below.)

Yet even without such common foodstuffs as tomatoes, potatoes, and rice there was a perhaps surprising variety in the staples that were eaten. The growing of grain was vitally important, for grains were used not only in the baking of bread (which the poor oftentimes subsisted on) but served as the thickening base for nearly every kind of stew-like browis, pottage, or frumenty. Bread even gives us the words for "Lady" and "Lord", for the Old English hlæfdige, 'kneader of bread', became Lady, and hlafward, 'keeper of the bread', became Lord.

And grains such as wheat, barley, rye, and oats were the basis for the brewing of ale. (Brewing used malted grains; grains such as barley which had been air dried, sprouted, then oven-dried.) Wheaten bread graced the tables of the high-born; coarser loaves of oat, barley, and rye (oftentimes adulterated with less-palatable seeds and even ground tree bark) fed the poor. We need to recall that 9th century ears of grain were far smaller than their modern counterparts which have been bred over many generations for large, plump, full heads.

Similarly, some domestic animals were smaller than those today. Many breeds of chickens were the size of today's bantam fowl, their eggs correspondingly smaller. Yet certain wild animals were larger. Solitary and very ill-tempered wild bulls roamed the hills beyond London as late as the 12th century. Wild boars were fierce, tough, and savvy fighters, claiming many a dog and huntsman with their sharp tusks.

Most diets were by necessity plant-based, and for the majority of folk meat was used sparingly as a flavouring agent. The slaughtering and roasting of a fatted calf or even an entire oxen which I depict in celebratory feasts were rare occasions even for the rich. Most meat was boiled or fried to capture every drop of precious fat and flavour; and roasting large animals consumed huge amounts of firewood. This is why the common morning and evening meal was browis, a combination of oats or barley with some meat broth, a kind of hearty porridge. This could be enlivened with the common vegetables of the day: shredded or cubed turnips, parsnips, radishes, beets, carrots and its relation, the little known today skirrets, onions, cabbage, and peas.

Greens such as lamb's lettuce, docks, parsley, purslane, bugloss, mallows, mints, and leeks were grown, gathered, and enjoyed in season, as were tonic Spring teas such as that made from the young leaves of the birch tree. Tansy leaves were ground in a mortar and pestle and stirred into beaten eggs and cooked like a frittata or omelette (just add Ham for a breakfast suitable for Dr. Seuss). Beans, chick-peas, and lentils were also grown during the period.

Butter, when available, was stirred into the browis to enrich it, and bread-and-butter is an ages-old enjoyment. Milk spoils quickly and went almost at once into butter or soft cheeses. Ewes' milk was commonly used for milk and to make both butter and cheese. The use of rennet (derived from the vell, or salted stomach lining, of calves) was understood, and that invaluable commodity salt was also used to cure and preserve cheese, as well as added to butter to increase its keeping qualities.

Ceramic floor tile from Westminster Abbey depicting fish, a sustaining food source for the resident monks

Regarding fish and shellfish, the many fast days of the early Church meant that even those who could afford meat often ate fish. (Lent was particularly challenging, as not even eggs could be eaten, and at a time of year when egg-laying was on the rise, and folk were hungry for any source of protein.) Certain types of fish which were wildly popular then have fallen out of favour – lampreys, and the river eel, for example. Baby eels were so relished that taxes and rent were paid in them. Fish were captured through the use of weirs (underwater traps consisting of stakes and netting), nets cast from boats, line fishing, and simply dipping a hooped fishing net into likely waters.

Successful line fishing, from the Boke (sic) of St Albans. Equipment and technique could not have changed much between the 9th and the 15th century.

All manner of things were collected or dug at low tide: winkles, whelks, sea snails, oysters (and Anglo-Saxon England was a rich source of pearls), mussels, clams, crayfish, crab. And the occasional leviathan washed ashore as well.

The Circle of Ceridwen Cookery Book(let)

A stranded whale became the property of the king, especially the tongue, considered a delicacy.

Fresh meat needed to be consumed quickly, and was most abundant during the slaughter month of Blodmonath,"blood-month", November, when livestock not strong or fit enough to be kept over Winter on limited fodder was killed and consumed in an orgy of feasting, the surplus being laid up for the lean months ahead. Meats were smoked, dried, salted, or laid up in brine (highly salted water). Farm animals were typically lean, and fat was highly prized. Sheep, cattle, goats, pigs, deer, and wild birds were all consumed by those who had the means to indulge; but almost every family kept a few hen-fowl and a pig, that invaluable garbage-disposal which assured that nothing at all went to waste. Bacon was as cherished then as it is now. Anglo-Saxons enjoyed the right to hunt upon their own lands; it was not until the advent of the

The Circle of Ceridwen Cookery Book(let)

Normans following the disaster of 1066 that all forest game became the property of the King and his henchmen. Poachers were regularly blinded or had their hands cut off in punishment. But let us turn our attention to something more pleasant: Sweets.

Natural sweeteners were few and far between. Fruits, fresh or dried, provided longed-for sweetness in earlier centuries, as did the naturally sweet vegetables parsnips, carrots, and skirrets. (But do remember that both parsnips and carrots have been bred to be as sweet as they are now.) Sugar from cane, grown originally in the tropical climes of Southeast Asia, would not spread to Britain until the 17th century slave plantations of the Caribbean produced cane in abundance; prior to this it was a luxury item on elite Elizabethan tables, consumed in lump form. Honey, beloved by all, was a treat, and in many parts a valuable trade commodity. Beeswax was just as valued for the naturally scented and clean-burning tapers that could be made from it, far superior to the ill-smelling and smoky tallow candles, made from animal fat, that the less-well-off used. (The truly poor had neither, and either sat in darkness – surely encouraging an 'early to bed' ethos – or used rush torches.) Honey was also the source of the potent and delicious alcoholic drink mead, made using the "washed" honey comb. Honey's preservative qualities were understood, and it was used, where available, to slather upon meat to keep it fresh longer, just as it was slathered on burns to soothe them. Honey has a natural antiseptic property which could not have been understood but was none the less known.

Bees heading out of their skeps, made by plaiting and sewing together straw coils.

Citrus, indispensable to us today, was unknown to our Anglo-Saxon forebears, but other fruit happily abounded: apples, pears, quinces, medlars, cherries, stone

The Circle of Ceridwen Cookery Book(let)

fruits like plums, all kinds of grapes and berries. Nutmeats such as walnuts, hickory nuts, and chestnuts were grown and gathered, and provided a health-some and hearty source of vegetable fat and protein.

Spices were fabulously valuable; the early 8th century English cleric the Venerable Bede died owning a small store of black pepper corns, which he carefully left to the grateful brother-monk recipients in his will. (Look kindly on that pepper mill when next you enter your own kitchen…it holds what was once a fortune!) Nearly all spices were held to have medicinal as well as culinary uses, increasingly their usefulness and value.

The next few pages will take you back in time on a culinary journey. If you've read the Saga novels you'll recognize some dishes at once, and I hope making them will transport you to the scenes and emotions of the books. And if you are completely new to the novels, getting to know the era through its foods is a magic portal in itself. I hope you enjoy the recipes, and use the journaling pages to write notes, amendments, and records of your own happy feasting.

Octavia Randolph

Visby, Gotland December 2019

The Circle of Ceridwen Cookery Book(let)

Honey Cakes

A specialty of Gunnvor the cook. Very easy to make, and addictive. Luckily Tindr is always glad to share his honey with friends.

Oven to 350 F / 180 C / Gas Mark 4

2 cups flour (you may use white flour or a mixture of whole meal/whole wheat and white)

1 tsp salt

3 tsp baking powder

5 Tbsp honey

4 Tbsp sweet (unsalted) butter

2 eggs

½ cup cream

Sift together the flour, salt, and baking powder. Dribble the tablespoons of honey over this, then drop in the butter, cut into small pieces. Toss so that the honey is covered by the flour mixture, then using your fingertips, rub the honey-butter into the flour so it is crumbly. (It will not be sticky – yet). Beat the eggs into the cream, and add to bowl; stir. (It will be sticky *now*.) Turn out onto generously floured board, sprinkle with more flour, and pat to about ½" – ¾" thickness. Using a drinking glass, cut into rounds, and lay on parchment-paper lined baking sheet. Bake for 12-15 minutes, until light golden and firm. Enjoy with butter, jam, or more honey. Makes 7 to 14, depending on your drinking glass. Mine is big.

Today we are blessed with baking powder, that Victorian combination of baking soda, cream of tartar, and cornstarch (created by British chemist Alfred Bird in 1843) which makes our cakes rise. But Gunnvor used "ash water", water in which the ashes of hardwood trees had been soaked. Hardwood ash contains sodium and potassium carbonate, sodium and potassium chloride, and calcium carbonate, and the strained water was added to quick breads such as cakes and biscuits to allow them to rise (the strained ashes could also be dried, ground down and used in powdered form).

Ashes were used for many other things, scouring and cleaning, for instance. Potassium carbonate is also known as potash, an alkali, and is naturally slippery or "soapy". When wet, ashes provide both the mild grit to scour, and the soapy quality of breaking down residual fats on cookware.

The Circle of Ceridwen Cookery Book(let)

When I made Honey Cakes

Who I served it to

How I made it my own

The Circle of Ceridwen Cookery Book(let)

The Circle of Ceridwen Cookery Book(let)

Baked Apples (or Pears)

Baked apples are wonderful, and the far less well known baked pears even more so, I think. Ceridwen has loved these since she was a girl at the Priory, and it was one of things she made with success at Tyrsborg when she was doing all the cooking, before the skilled Gunnvor came to them. A great treat for breakfast, but luscious enough for a fine dessert.

Oven to 350 F / 180 C / Gas Mark 4

Your favourite pie pastry for a three crust pie (by which I mean, take your two crust recipe and scale it up by 50%, so you will have enough pastry to cover six pieces of fruit)

6 firm tart apples, or firm pears

4 Tbsp honey

1 tsp ground cinnamon (because you are rich)

12 walnut halves

2 Tbsp butter

Core, but do not peel the apples (or pears). Divide the pie crust into six balls, and roll each ball out on a floured surface thinly enough to wrap each apple in. Warm the honey slightly so that it is fluid, and stir in the cinnamon (as you do not need to save it for your daughter's dowry).

The Circle of Ceridwen Cookery Book(let)

Place each apple in the centre of the pie pastry. Drop a couple of walnut halves into each hollowed core, pour a small amount of the honey/cinnamon mixture in after, and then add 1 tsp butter to each. Wrap the pastry crust up around the apple, securing it well by twisting or merely pinching it in place. Rustic is beautiful! Place in a rimmed, buttered baking dish and bake for 45 minutes for pears, and 50 to 55 minutes for apples. The crust should be golden brown. Serve warm as is, or with cream.

A wide variety of things, both sweet and savoury, were baked in pastry during the Anglo-Saxon period. A pastry casing holds moisture and flavour in, and can be delicious on its own account, or in the case of a coarser pastry covering, broken away from the edible interior, and enjoyed by the family pig. Sometimes even clay, moulded about the food, was used, in the case of sea birds baked gutted but with feathers intact. The feathers were to have been pulled off, stuck in the "fired" clay, after baking...

The Circle of Ceridwen Cookery Book(let)

When I made Baked Apples (or Pears)

Who I served it to

How I made it my own

The Circle of Ceridwen Cookery Book(let)

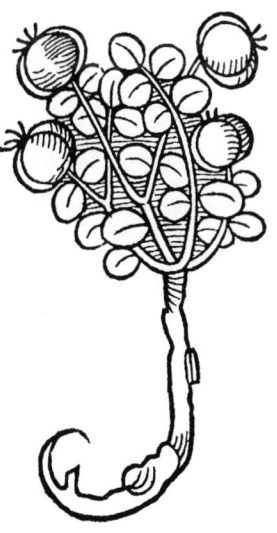

The Circle of Ceridwen Cookery Book(let)

Barley Browis

Admittedly simple but truly satisfying. Browis, a thick stew-like porridge, was the everyday meal for most folk in the 9th century. Endlessly adaptable to the grains, vegetables and meats at hand, it was filling, easy to make, and nourishing. I like pearl barley, but whole oats can be used with equal authenticity as well. The barley needs to soak for several hours before you cook it, so keep this in mind.

1 cup pearl barley

3 cups broth (meat or vegetable)

2 cups mixed vegetables, any combination of carrots, parsnips, beets, turnips, onions,…diced, or in small slices

4 Tbsp butter

Salt (and, as you are rich) black pepper, to taste

Rinse the barley in a fine mesh strainer, and then cover with water and let sit and soak at room temperature for several hours or overnight. Drain and rinse the barley. In a large heavy-bottomed soup pot melt 1 Tbsp of the butter over low heat, and add the drained and rinsed barley, stirring well so all the pearls are coated with a light coating of butter. Let it sit there over low heat, stirring occasionally, while you address the vegetables, peeling them and dicing or slicing them.

The Circle of Ceridwen Cookery Book(let)

After the barley has been toasting for 5-8 minutes, add the broth to the pot, and turn to the heat to high. Cover and bring to a boil, then reduce heat to medium low, taking care not to let it overboil and make a mess (you may wish to set the cover a little to one side to prevent this).

In a heavy-bottomed skillet melt the butter over medium heat, and add the sliced or cubed vegetables. Sauté the vegetables, moving them around frequently with a wooden spoon, until they begin to brown a bit, and grow slightly tender, about 5 minutes. Scrape them and the butter and juices in their pan into the soup pot with the simmering barley, and cook for 15 to 20 minutes, depending on how chewy you like your browis. Add salt and pepper to taste, and if you'd like the browis to be soupier, add more broth. Makes 4 1½ cup servings.

- ❖ To enrich or vary the browis, add a cup of cooked, shredded or cubed venison, rabbit, fowl, or any other meat, at the end of cooking.
- ❖ Dried or fresh herbs such as thyme and sage may be sautéed with the diced vegetables, or fresh parsley chopped up and stirred in just before serving.

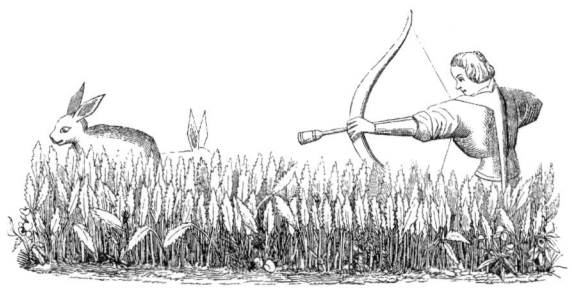

The Circle of Ceridwen Cookery Book(let)

When I made Barley Browis

Who I served it to

How I made it my own

The Circle of Ceridwen Cookery Book(let)

The Circle of Ceridwen Cookery Book(let)

Honey-glazed Carrots and Parsnips

This makes a dramatically pretty dish, the snowy parsnips contrasting with the orange of the carrots. I like to use smaller carrots (not peeled baby carrots, but smaller, slender whole carrots) and leave them whole. It's hard to find truly small parsnips, so you may have to slice them lengthwise in half, or even quarters. (If they are very large don't hesitate to dig out the hard pith in the middle.) Peeled sliced beets, red or golden, make a nice addition/substitution, too. Put them in the pan when you start the carrots.

Root vegetables such as these were set in iron or soapstone pans, with hot wood coals heaped up outside the pan to the rim, and demanded little attention from the busy cook except an occasional stir to keep them from sticking.

1 pound slender carrots, scrubbed or lightly peeled, left whole

1 pound parsnips, scrubbed or peeled, cut in half lengthwise, or quarters if truly large

3 Tbsp butter (more if needed)

1 Tbsp honey

6 mint leaves, lightly torn or chopped

Melt the butter under medium low heat in a large heavy skillet. Add the peeled or scrubbed carrots first, as they take longer to cook than the parsnips. Push the carrots about in the butter until they are coated, and after 5 minutes, add the parsnips. Cover the skillet and keep it over medium-low heat, stirring every once in a while to check they are not browning too quickly. It will take about 20 minutes for them to be tender. Dribble in the honey and give the vegetables a final stir to make sure all are anointed. Remove to a serving dish and snip or tear the mint leaves over all. Easily serves six, unless you are a rabbit.

Mint is such a strong grower it's practically a weed. In fact in my garden it is a weed, which is why I like to use it every chance I can. Its cooling spiciness is the perfect foil for the sweetness of the vegetables.

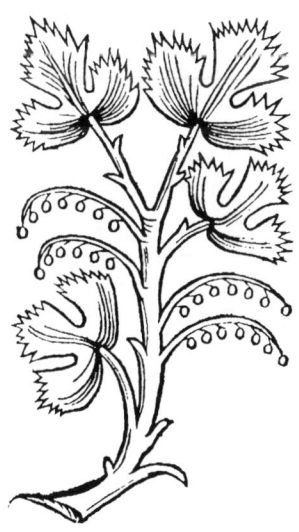

The Circle of Ceridwen Cookery Book(let)

When I made Honey-glazed Carrots and Parsnips

Who I served it to

How I made it my own

The Circle of Ceridwen Cookery Book(let)

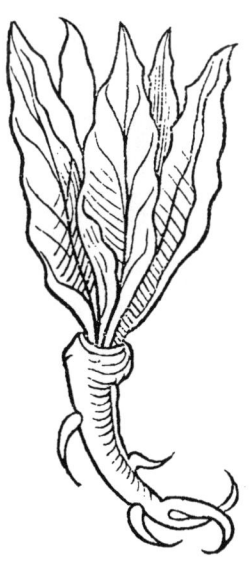

The Circle of Ceridwen Cookery Book(let)

Oat Griddle Cakes

The nourishing cakes that Gudrid and Sparrow griddled up at Rannveig's brew house to feed everyone after the fire. Do not be deterred by the steel cut oats, they take only 20 – 25 minutes to cook and are worth the wait. (Or you can make the oats the night before, and pull them out of the 'fridge.) These griddle cakes are lighter, and more delicious, than you may expect. Perfect for breakfast, hearty tea, or accompanying a late night supper.

2 cups cooked steel cut oats

1 cup flour (for heartier cakes use whole meal/whole wheat flour, or a mixture)

2 tsp baking power

1 cup whole milk

1 egg

2 Tbsp melted butter, slightly cooled

3 Tbsp honey

½ tsp salt

¼ cup raisins or dried currants or chopped dried cherries or blueberries (optional)

Have ready a heavy cast-iron fry pan or griddle, and butter with which to grease it.

The Circle of Ceridwen Cookery Book(let)

Whisk the butter and milk together in a medium size bowl and add the egg and honey, whisking well. Add the cooked oats and stir, then add the flour, baking powder, and salt. Add dried fruit if you are using. Stir until just nicely combined. If the batter is very thick, thin with a bit more milk.

Heat your iron fry pan or griddle until medium hot to hot; you will soon find how much heat it takes to toast the cakes without scorching them. Grease the pan well with butter, and drop the oak cakes by large spoonfuls onto the hot surface. When the cake is brown on the bottom, flip and cook the other side. Serve unadorned, or with honey, applesauce, or jam. Makes 12 to14 4" cakes, enough for four hungry fire-fighters.

Oats are so hardy they grow well in even wet and cold environments, and so of necessity became a beloved staple in places like the North Country and the Scottish Highlands. And of course, what would our horses do without them?

The Circle of Ceridwen Cookery Book(let)

When I made Oat Griddle Cakes

Who I served it to

How I made it my own

The Circle of Ceridwen Cookery Book(let)

The Circle of Ceridwen Cookery Book(let)

Venison Pie with Juniper Berries

The very same pie that Gunnvor the cook bakes up for Ceridwen and Sidroc. Filling, delicious, and atmospheric. Juniper wood was prized as a wood over which to smoke haunches of pig and deer.

Oven to 350 F / 180 C / Gas Mark 4

Your favourite pie pastry for a two crust pie

12 oz (340 grams, or about 2 cups) cooked ground venison, chicken, turkey, pork, or beef, well drained; (or seasoned tofu crumbles, which is what I use, being vegetarian)

¾ cup carrots, thinly sliced or in small dice

1 Tbsp raisins, chopped

3 juniper berries, crushed slightly in a mortar and pestle

A 5" sprig each of fresh rosemary and thyme, stems removed, rosemary leaves chopped if large; *or* one fresh sage leaf, snipped into lengths, and a small sprig of thyme, stems removed

A grinding of black pepper (if you are rich)

1 egg, beaten into ½ cup of ale (or apple juice, or broth)

Roll out your pie dough and divide in half. Line a 9" pie plate with one crust, or use two 5" diameter oven-proof ramekins. In a medium size bowl combine the crumbled protein, carrots, raisins, juniper berries, herbs, and pepper. Pour the ale into a small bowl and beat the egg into it with a whisk. Add to protein/vegetable mixture and blend. Spoon into pie pan or ramekins, and top with top crust. Create a couple of vents for steam to escape by making small slashes in the crust with a sharp knife. Bake in bottom third of oven for 35 minutes or until crust is light golden brown. Serve warm or at room temperature. Satisfies four hearty appetites.

The Circle of Ceridwen Cookery Book(let)

When I made Venison Pie with Juniper Berries

Who I served it to

How I made it my own

The Circle of Ceridwen Cookery Book(let)

The Circle of Ceridwen Cookery Book(let)

Fish Stew with Leeks and Lentils

This makes a pretty soup, with the red or yellow lentils, orange carrots, and bright green parsley peeking out from the milky broth. This sort of fish stew, with dried peas, beans, or lentils, was a common Anglo-Saxon preparation, and like most fish soups or chowders, the flavour even improves the next day.. Parsley is mentioned in every single existing fish dish of the era, so don't forget it!

2 Tbsp butter

2 leeks, white and palest green part only, thinly sliced

4 medium or 2 large carrots, sliced

½ cup chopped parsley, loosely packed

½ cup of ale (you may substitute water or fish stock for this)

1 ½ cup of water

1 cup red or yellow lentils, picked over and rinsed

1 pound/ 450 grams firm white fleshed fish, such as cod, halibut, haddock, plaice/flounder, striped bass, cut into small pieces

1 ½ cups whole milk, at room temperature

Salt and black pepper, to taste

A grating of nutmeg (if you are very, very rich)

Melt butter in a large, heavy bottomed soup pot, and sauté sliced carrots for 5 minutes over medium heat, stirring frequently so nothing sticks to the bottom. Add leeks and sauté for a few minutes more.the parsley, ale, water, and lentils, and bring to a boil. Reduce heat to a simmer, setting the cover aside to prevent over-boiling, if needed. Stir occasionally, and after 8 -10 minutes taste the lentils for doneness. They should still be slightly firm but just on the cusp of tenderness.

Add the fish pieces, and raise the heat for 3-4 minutes. Lower the heat and stir in the milk, simmering gently a couple minutes longer until the fish is flaky. Season to taste with salt and pepper, and a grating of nutmeg, if desired. Serves 4 as a main course or 8 as a soup course. Add more milk if needed to thin to desired consistency.

The Abbot of Cirencester, Alexander Neckam (1157-1217) wrote down his recipe for Fish Stew: "Plaice boiled. Take a plaice, and draw him in the side by the head; And make a sauce of water, parsley, salt, and a little ale; and when it beginneth to boil, skim it clean, and cast it thereto, and let seeth." Although Alexander lived after the end of the Anglo-Saxon age, his description is very similar to those handed down in earlier leech books (books on healing).

The Circle of Ceridwen Cookery Book(let)

When I made Fish Stew with Leeks and Lentils

Who I served it to

How I made it my own

The Circle of Ceridwen Cookery Book(let)

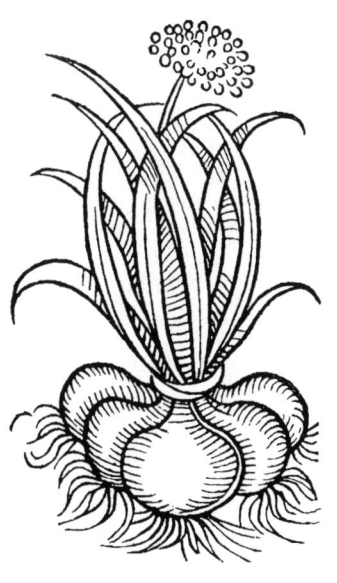

The Circle of Ceridwen Cookery Book(let)

Roasted Fish with Green Sauce

All manner of raw green herbs were eaten in Anglo-Saxon England, giving welcome freshness, brightness, and minerals to cooked dishes. "Green Sauce", an almost pesto-like condiment, was both spooned onto roasted or baked fish, and stirred into fish stew. Green Sauce could be as simple as finely minced parsley, mixed with bread crumbs, salt, and verjuice or mild vinegar; or a more complex flavour base combining parsley, mint, costmary (a sweet-smelling minty herb I am partial to, but one hard to find outside of one's own garden), dill, sage, dittany, and black pepper, to which finely ground bread crumbs, ale, or verjuice/vinegar was added.

Your favourite firm, white fleshed fish, either grilled, baked, or broiled

For the Green Sauce:

Equal amounts mint, parsley, and dill (one small bunch of each will make enough to cover a fish serving four)

½ cup of bread crumbs, made from a slice of good bread, lightly toasted and crumbled

3 Tbsp verjuice (see below), or 2 Tbsp red wine vinegar plus 1 Tbsp water

2 Tbsp melted butter, slightly cooled

The Circle of Ceridwen Cookery Book(let)

Salt and black pepper (because, as I keep reminding you, you are rich and can afford it)

Carefully wash the herbs, freeing them from all grit, and cut away larger stems. Mince together very finely, crush in a mortar and pestle, or place in food processor and pulse a moment until chopped, then pulse again with the verjuice (or vinegar/water) and melted butter. Add the bread crumbs and pulse briefly. (Add a bit more melted butter if you'd like a silkier consistency.) Season with salt and pepper to taste, and serve either under or spooned over the cooked fish.

Verjuice or verjus, literally "green juice", is the juice pressed from unripe grapes, or lacking them, crab apples. It makes a milder form of vinegar, with little bite but a pleasing tang. It is easy to make at home, if a trifle time consuming, for those with a source of unripe grapes handy. Good instructions are easily found online.

You may substitute apple cider vinegar for the red wine vinegar, but as it is sharper in flavour, use it in a 1:1 ratio with water.

The Circle of Ceridwen Cookery Book(let)

When I made Roasted Fish with Green Sauce

Who I served it to

How I made it my own

The Circle of Ceridwen Cookery Book(let)

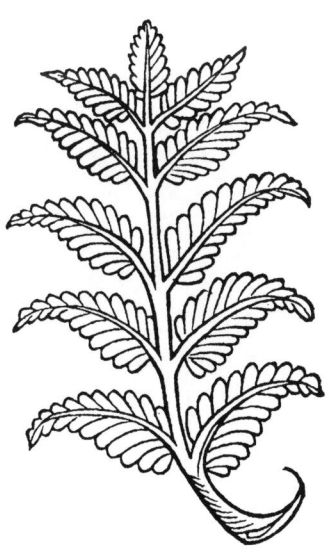

The Circle of Ceridwen Cookery Book(let)

Roast Fowl, Two Ways

A delicacy prepared both at Kilton in Wessex, and at Tyrsborg, on Gotland. This bird is basted in a mixture of honey and red wine vinegar. The Kilton version uses rosemary, that piney, resinous herb we think of being quintessentially Mediterranean, but the Romans brought rosemary over to Britain early, where it adapted well. The Tyrsborg version, in colder Gotland, uses sage and thyme.

Oven to 425 F / 220 C / Gas Mark 7

1 whole roasting chicken, 4- 6 lbs (2 to 3 kilos), washed and patted dry

For Roast Fowl, Kilton-style:

1 5" sprig of fresh rosemary, stem removed; if leaves are very large, chop them slightly

2 Tbsp of butter, softened

For Roast Fowl, Tyrsborg-style:

3 fresh sage leaves, sliced into narrow lengths

1 4" sprig of fresh thyme, stem removed

2 Tbsp of butter, softened

For both versions:

½ cup red wine vinegar

¼ cup water

1 Tbsp honey

Salt and black pepper, because you deserve it

Place the chicken in a roasting pan. Combine the vinegar and water and warm the honey in it slightly. Mash the chosen herbs into the softened butter, and using your fingers gently pull the skin on the breasts away from the meat, trying not to tear it. Press the herbed butter between the skin and flesh of the breast, pushing it in as deeply and evenly as you can. Pour a bit of the vinegar/water/honey mixture in after, between the skin and flesh (a bulb baster is handy here), and a bit more over the skin. Pour about a ¼ of the vinegar mixture into the breast cavity, reserving the remaining for basting. Sprinkle salt and pepper over all.

Roast for 20 minutes, then baste with the remaining vinegar/water/honey mixture. (A piece of buttered foil placed over the breast at this point will prevent it from over-roasting as we wait for the rest of the bird to be done.) Bake another 25 minutes, until a meat thermometer inserted at the thigh reads 165 F / 74 C. The skin will be a beautiful reddish shade, and the meat tender and flavourful.

The Circle of Ceridwen Cookery Book(let)

When I made Roast Fowl Two Ways

Who I served it to

How I made it my own

The Circle of Ceridwen Cookery Book(let)

The Circle of Ceridwen Cookery Book(let)

Lavender–scented Pudding

A delightful and rich soufflé-like pudding, redolent of lavender. Gunnvor made this at Yule up at Tyrsborg, having carefully preserved the eggs, buried in a barrel of cold ashes. Of course she used Tindr's honey. And a birch twig whisk to beat those egg whites. But you get to use an electric mixer…

Oven to 350 F / 180 C / Gas Mark 4 *Allow three hours for the lavender to steep in the milk before making*

1 cup whole milk

2 Tbsp dried lavender flowers, if possible from the garden of someone you love

¼ cup flour

6 Tbsp honey

1 Tbsp melted butter

3 eggs, separated

Butter the inside of six 6 oz ramekins, and dust lightly with flour.

Pour the milk into a small saucepan and add the lavender flowers. Bring to a simmer, stirring, and turn off the heat and allow the lavender to steep in the milk at room temperature for three hours. Strain, discarding the lavender, but saving the milk.

The Circle of Ceridwen Cookery Book(let)

Combine 2 Tbsp of the honey with the melted butter, and stir into the flour. In another bowl. whisk the egg yolks and strained milk together, and then add the honey-butter-flour mix to this and whisk until smooth.

Beat the egg whites at medium speed until soft peaks form, and then add the remaining 4 Tbsp honey in increments, increasing speed to high until the whites form stiff peaks. Take about a third of the beaten whites and stir them into the egg yolk/milk/flour mixture, and then add the rest of the egg whites, gently folding in.

Pour into the prepared ramekins so they are about ¾ full, and set on a baking sheet. Place into preheated oven. Bake for 15 - 20 minutes, or until risen high and golden brown. Allow to rest on a rack for a few minutes before serving warm.

Impressive and delicious, a sweet memory of Summer any time of year. (Any left over is equally good, even cold and deflated, for breakfast. Now how would I know that?...)

The Circle of Ceridwen Cookery Book(let)

When I made Lavender-scented Pudding

Who I served it to

How I made it my own

The Circle of Ceridwen Cookery Book(let)

The Circle of Ceridwen Cookery Book(let)

I hope you have enjoyed your culinary adventure in the 9th century! Come to octavia.net or my Facebook page and let me know what you liked best...

Wish to dive deeper into the foods of the era? There are fine books available:

Leechcraft: Early English Charms Plantlore and Healing Stephen Pollington, Anglo-Saxon Books 2000

Food and Drink in Britain From the Stone age to the 19th Century, C. Anne Wilson, Academy Chicago Publishers, 1991

A Handbook of Anglo-Saxon Food: Processing and Consumption Ann Hagen, Anglo-Saxon Books 1992

Tastes of Anglo-Saxon England, Mary Savelli, Anglo-Saxon Books 2002

The Circle of Ceridwen Cookery Book(let)

The Circle of Ceridwen Saga:

The Circle of Ceridwen: Book One

Ceridwen of Kilton: Book Two

The Claiming: Book Three

The Hall of Tyr: Book Four

Tindr: Book Five

Silver Hamer, Golden Cross: Book Six

Sidroc the Dane

Dinner entertainment is always welcome.
Enjoy your feast!

The Circle of Ceridwen Cookery Book(let)

That night when we camped I worked up the feast I had promised. I boiled the peas and we ate them first, sweet as honey. The dock and sorrel and plantain leaves I stewed with shreds of the smoked stag, and made broth which I bottled in our jugs for the morrow. I added barley to what remained and boiled it until we had a thick browis. I sprinkled upon it a bit of salt from my twist, and it made a dish fit for those in a timber hall.

-What Ceridwen cooks up for Gyric and herself in the forest during their flight from Four Stones to Kilton, from Book One of *The Circle of Ceridwen*

For the naming-feast the oaken board had been massed with all the early Spring bounty the burh of Kilton could provide, and our first cup had been precious wine from Frankland. We had feasted on crackling-skinned rock doves, bitterns, and grouse, and bowls of thick browis, steaming with leeks and turnips; and then taken bright ale with platters of dried apples and cherries stewed in tart verjuice. All was of delicious savour, and as I was always hungry now that I was suckling Ceric, I ate my fill and more.

-Ceridwen describing the Naming feast to celebrate her son Ceric's birth, from *Ceridwen of Kilton*

The Circle of Ceridwen Cookery Book(let)

The Welcome Feast that Godwin had ordered was rich as any in Kilton's memory. First wine was poured, and golden mead, gift of the bee; and then followed clear brown ale, sparkling from long-standing in Modwynn's ale house. Milk-calfs and young pig set off with leeks, turnips, skirrits, and late greens followed plate after plate of roast sea fish. Frumentys, rich with milk and thickened with boiled barley and beaten eggs preceded bowls of honeyed dried elderberries and cherries. Fresh pears, so juicy that they spurted at the knife's touch, came last. All this was set off by scores of hot loaves of white bread, crusted and seeded and steaming from the ovens.

Sidroc sat at Godwin's right hand, and Gyric at Godwin's left; and then sat I, and then Modwynn, flanking our honoured guest...

-The feast at Kilton in which all five main characters – Ceridwen, Gyric, Godwin, Ælfwyn, and Sidroc – are seated together, from *Ceridwen of Kilton*

The Circle of Ceridwen Cookery Book(let)

Liquid Conversions

Liquids

U.S.	Metric
1 tsp	5 ml
1 Tbs	15 ml
2 Tbs	30 ml
3 Tbs	45 ml
1/4 cup	60 ml
1/3 cup	75 ml
1/2 cup	120 ml
2/3 cup	150 ml
3/4 cup	180 ml
1 cup	240 ml
1 1/4 cups	300 ml
1 1/3 cups	325 ml
1 1/2 cups	350 ml
1 2/3 cups	375 ml
1 3/4 cups	400 ml
2 cups (1 pint)	475 ml
3 cups	720 ml
4 cups (1 quart)	945 ml

The Circle of Ceridwen Cookery Book(let)

Weight Conversions

Weights

U.S./U.K.	Metric
1/2 oz	14 g
1 oz	28 g
1 1/2 oz	43 g
2 oz	57 g
3 oz	85 g
3 1/2 oz	100 g
4 oz	113 g
5 oz	142 g
6 oz	170 g
7 oz	200 g
8 oz	227 g
9 oz	255 g
10 oz	284 g
11 oz	312 g
12 oz	340 g
13 oz	368 g
14 oz	400 g
15 oz	425 g
16 oz (1 lb)	454 g

Made in United States
Orlando, FL
29 May 2024